A Balancing Act

Dynamic Nature and Her Ecosystems

Ecology for Kids | Science Kids 3rd Grade | Children's Environment Books

First Edition, 2020

Published in the United States by Speedy Publishing LLC, 40 E Main Street, Newark, Delaware 19711 USA.

Baby Professor Books are available at special discounts when purchased in bulk for industrial and sales-promotional use. For details contact our Special Sales Team at Speedy Publishing LLC, 40 E Main Street, Newark, Delaware 19711 USA. Telephone (888) 248-4521 Fax: (210) 519-4043.

10 9 8 7 6 * 5 4 3 2 1

Print Edition: 9781541949201
Digital Edition: 9781541951006
Hardcover Edition: 9781541980051

See the world in pictures. Build your knowledge in style.
www.speedypublishing.com

Table of Contents

Balance is an important part of life. You have probably heard of the work-life balance, or about eating a balanced diet. If we work too much, we can hurt ourselves. However, if we never work, we will also be unhealthy. With food, it can be nice to eat cake every so often, but if we eat it everyday, it can cause us to become overweight and malnourished.

Balance is an important part of life.

Ecosystems rely on a balance to be healthy.

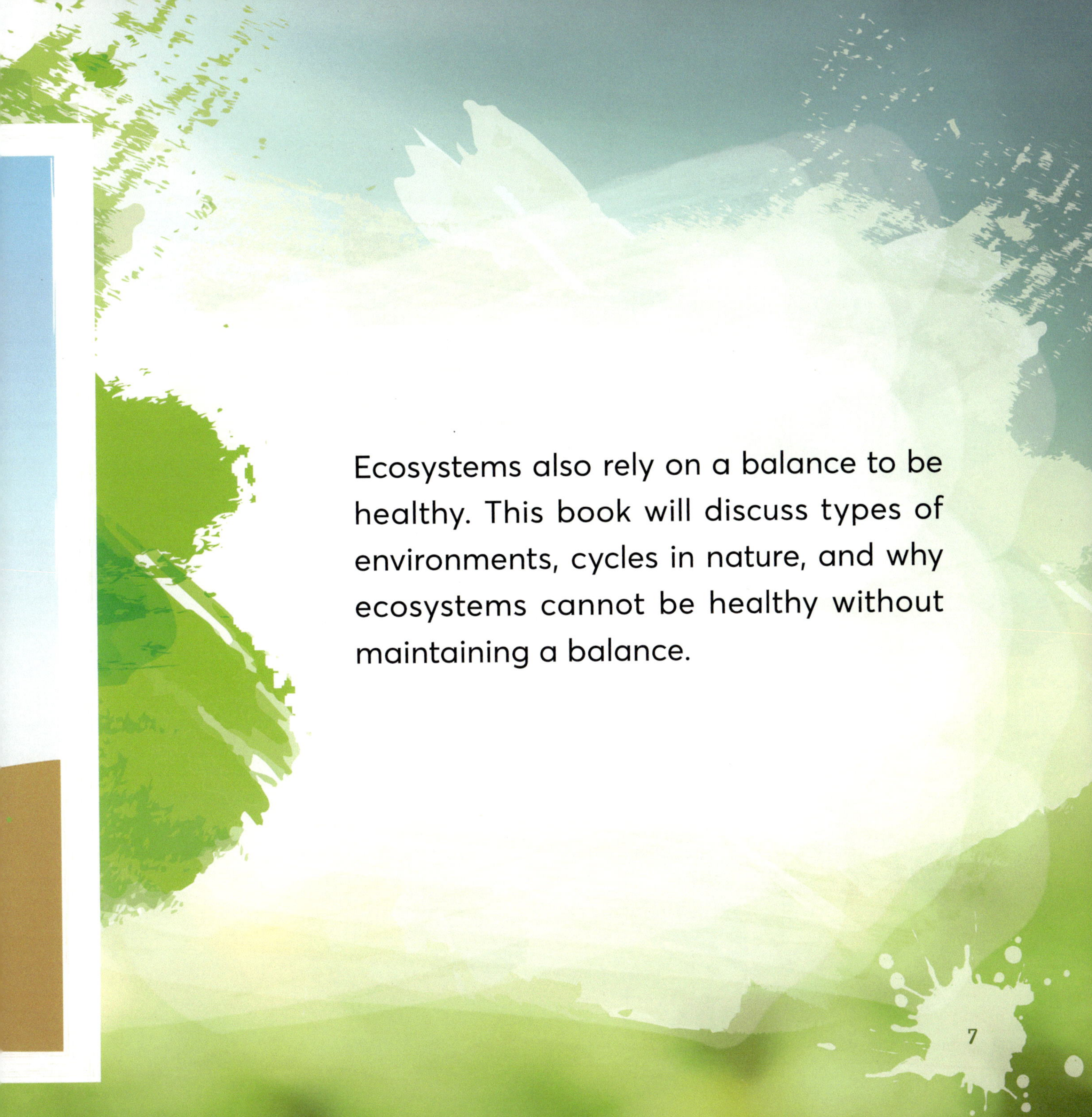

Ecosystems also rely on a balance to be healthy. This book will discuss types of environments, cycles in nature, and why ecosystems cannot be healthy without maintaining a balance.

Chapter One:
Types of Ecosystems

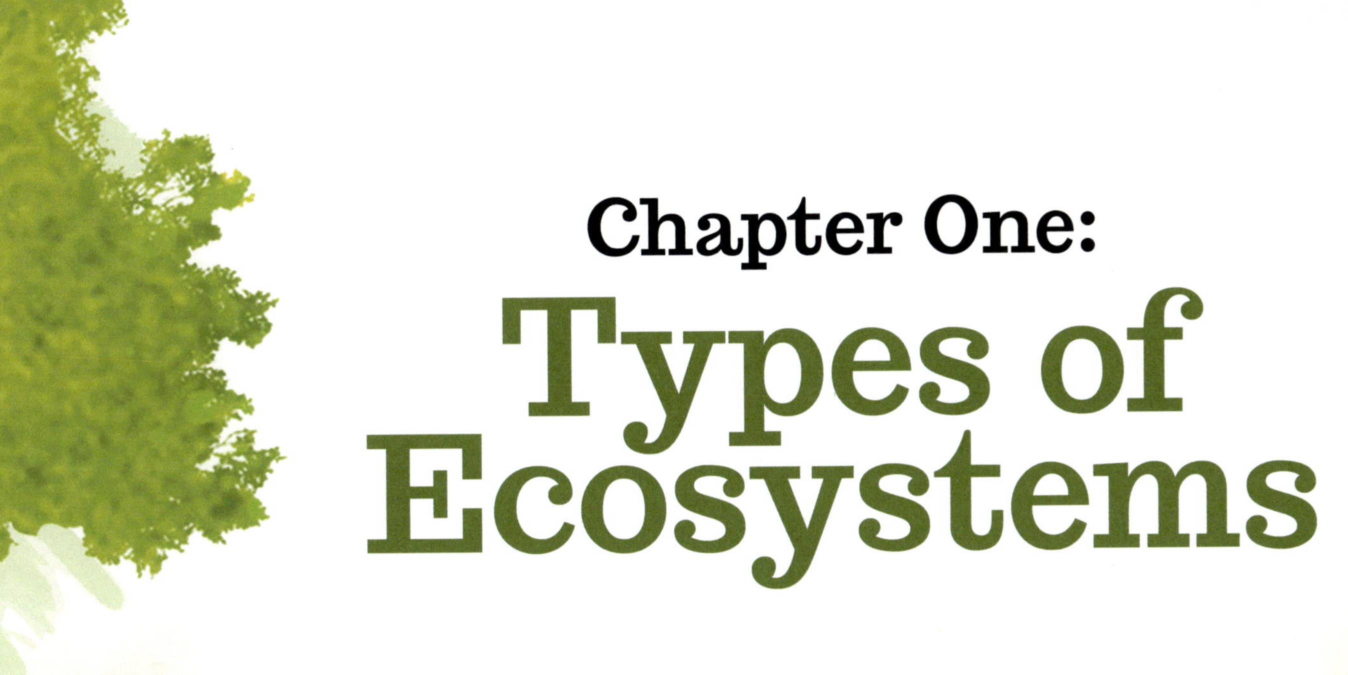

An ecosystem is made up of the interactions of species and their environment in a specific area. This includes all the organisms, both plants and animals, and anything else within an area. The living parts of an ecosystem can be called biotic, while the non-living is called abiotic.

An ecosystem is made up of the interactions of species and their environment in a specific area.

It is important that the inhabitants of an ecosystem live in the right climate.

It is important that the inhabitants of an ecosystem live in the right climate. They need to have water, food, and shelter. If any of these conditions are lacking, the ecosystem will change or life in the area will die out.

Ecosystems can be divided into two broad categories: Terrestrial and aquatic.

Terrestrial Ecosystems:

Terrestrial is from Latin and it refers to things that are on land. Any ecosystem that is not found in water can be said to be terrestrial. Some common classifications of terrestrial ecosystems are taiga, deciduous forests, grasslands, and tundra. A taiga is a kind of forest that is full of conifers and it is found in very cold areas. Conifers are trees that produce cones and have needle-like leaves. A quite common type of conifer is the pine tree.

Taiga forests of Oulanka National Park in Kuusamo, Finland

The tundra is often thought of as a cold wasteland. Little can grow in a tundra and it receives little sunlight. Tundra are typically found in the far north. You know you have entered the tundra when you have passed the tree line of the taiga.

Anadyr tundra, Chukotka, Siberia, Far East Russia

Deciduous forests are forests that are found in warmer areas. The weather and climate are often more seasonal in such regions. A deciduous tree is a type of tree that sheds its leaves for winter.

Deciduous forest in Heidelberg, Germany

Open Prairie Grasslands in Tibetan Amdo Region of Central China.

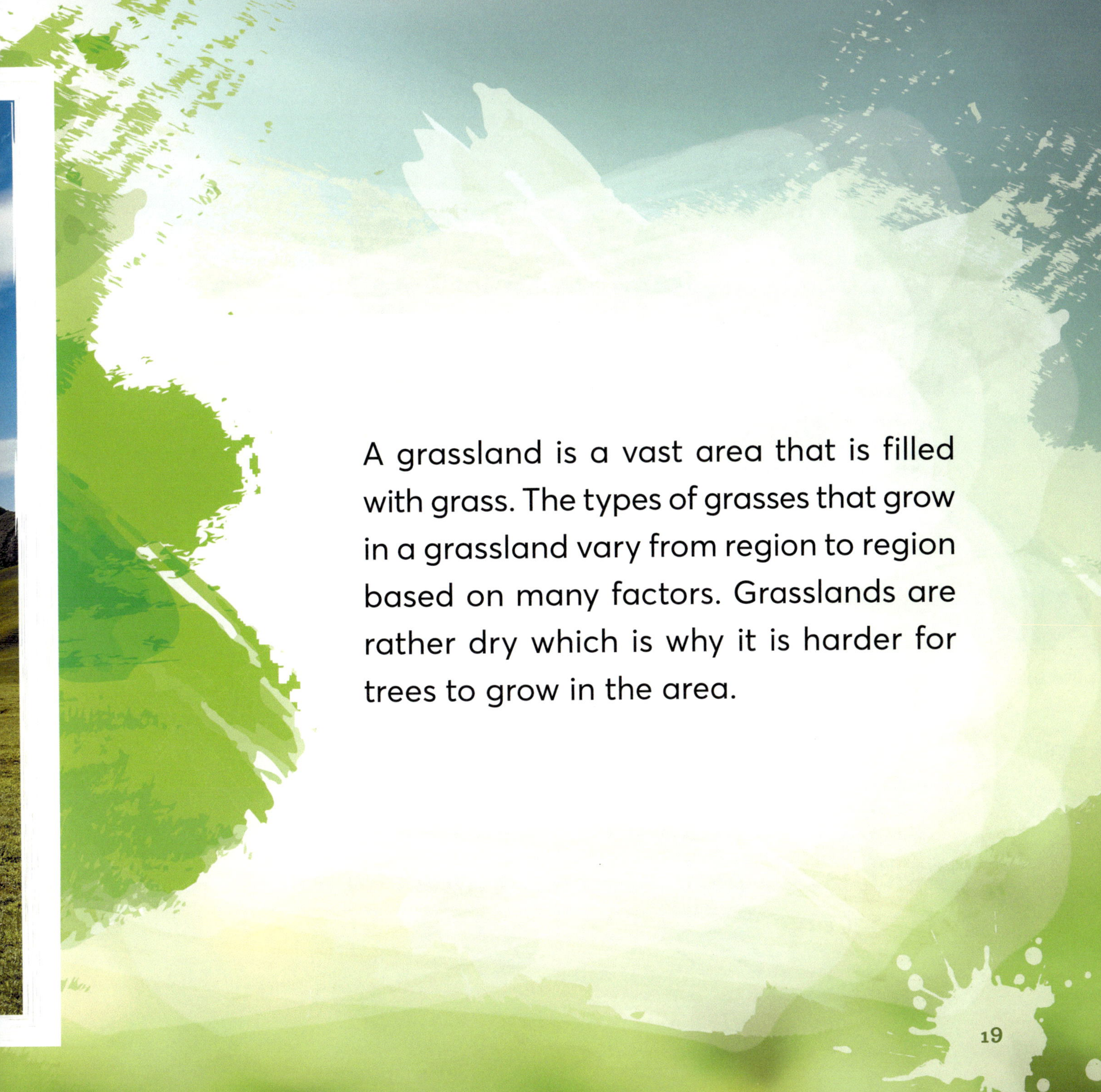

A grassland is a vast area that is filled with grass. The types of grasses that grow in a grassland vary from region to region based on many factors. Grasslands are rather dry which is why it is harder for trees to grow in the area.

Aquatic Ecosystems:

Aquatic comes from the Latin word for water. Hence, an aquatic ecosystem is an ecosystem that is found in the water. Aquatic ecosystems can either be freshwater or saltwater, also known as marine.

Marine ecosystems are not necessarily in the ocean. They can also be in places that receive salt water. Estuaries are places where rivers run into the ocean. Mangroves are swamps that become flooded by salt water at high tides. There are also salt marshes. They are areas like grasslands that can become flooded by saltwater from the ocean.

Mangrove Swamp in Tecolutla, Veracruz, Mexico

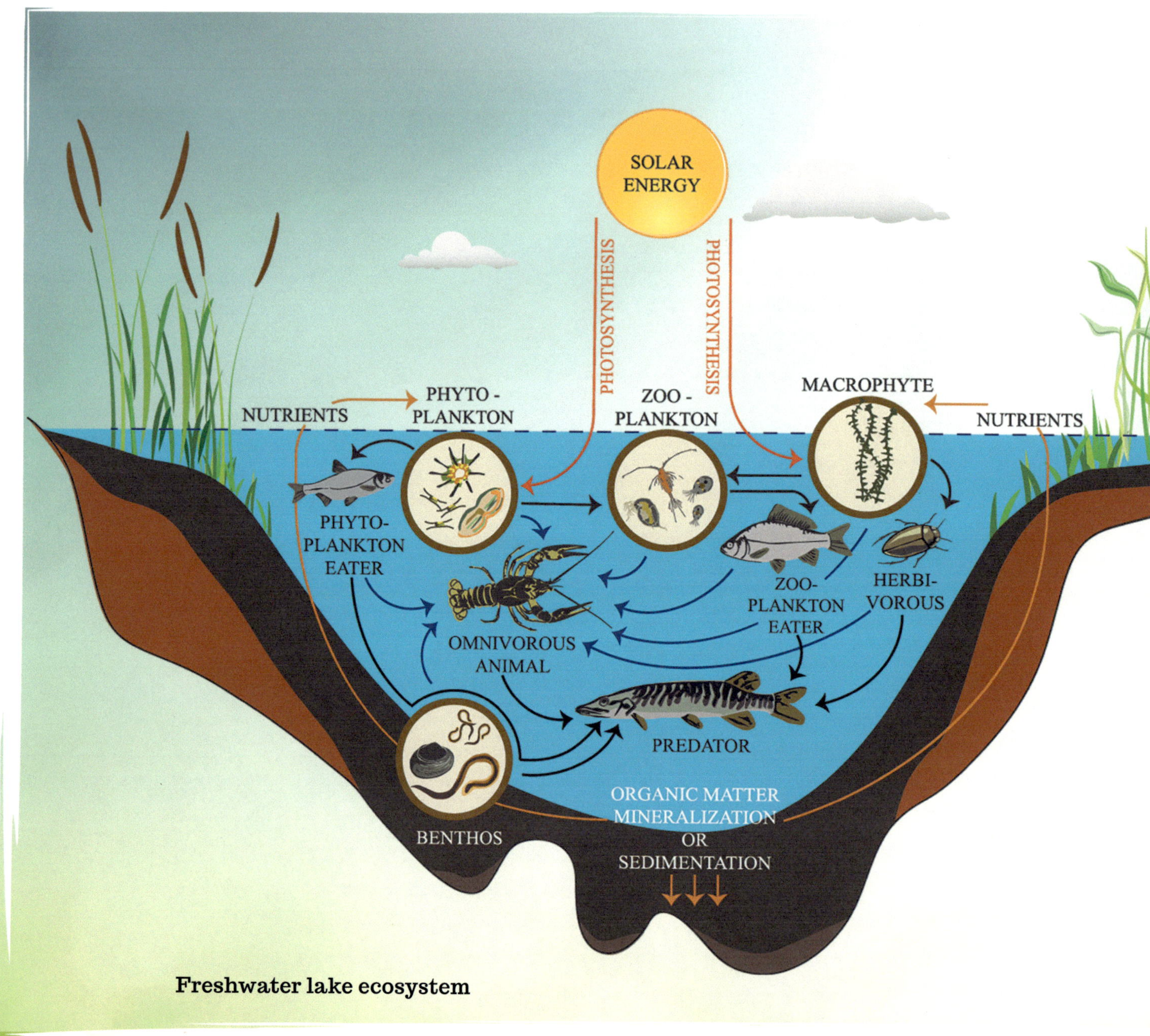

Freshwater lake ecosystem

Freshwater ecosystems are more well-known. They are rivers, lakes, springs, and other areas inland where water might collect. They can be classified by how the water flows, the amount of water, the amount of nutrients the water has, as well as temperature and quantity of sunlight.

Chapter Two: Nature's Cycles

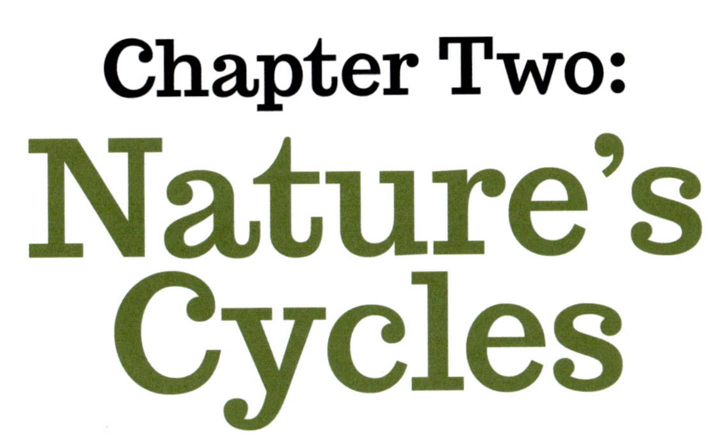

We are often told to recycle. This is because resources are finite. There is only so much water, gas, metal, and other things on the Earth. To make sure that we do not run out, we need to reuse the things we no longer need. In nature, there are several cycles that "recycle" naturally. These cycles help maintain the balance to sustain a healthy ecosystem.

REUSE

USE THINGS MORE THAN ONCE
REPAIR
REGIFT!

RECYCLE

SEPARATE WASTE MATERIALS
COMPOST
CHOOSE RECYCLABLE!

AVOID WASTE!
BUY LESS
CONSERVE WATER

REDUCE

To make sure that we do not run out, we need to reuse the things we no longer need.

HETEROTROPH

PRODUCERS

Produce their own food for energy. Use Photosynthesis or Chemosynthesis

CONSUMERS

Eat other organisms to get proteins and energy

Sun

Grass
Photosynthesis

Grasshopper

Toad

Plants

Some bacteria

Algae

Animals

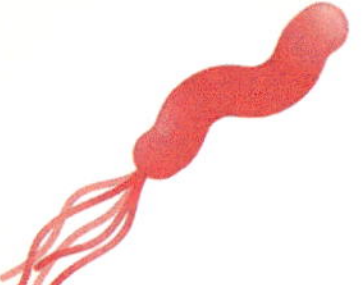

Most bacteria

Fungi

The Nutrient Cycle:

Every ecosystem is made up of three different things: autotrophs, heterotrophs, and inorganic matter. Autotrophs are creatures that produce their own energy. Heterotrophs consume or use up energy. Inorganic matter refers to things that are not living but help to sustain life.

Most autotrophs are plants. Plants lie at the bottom of the food chain since they can use energy from the Sun to make their own food. They produce the energy for the heterotrophs to consume. Animals, whether they eat plants or animals, are heterotrophs. They cannot make their own energy, so they must eat to break down energy from other sources. Eating also provides them with nutrition that they need.

Properly, a food chain not only shows who eats whom, but shows where the energy goes. Since energy is not perfectly transferred from one animal to another through eating, there will generally be more prey than predators.

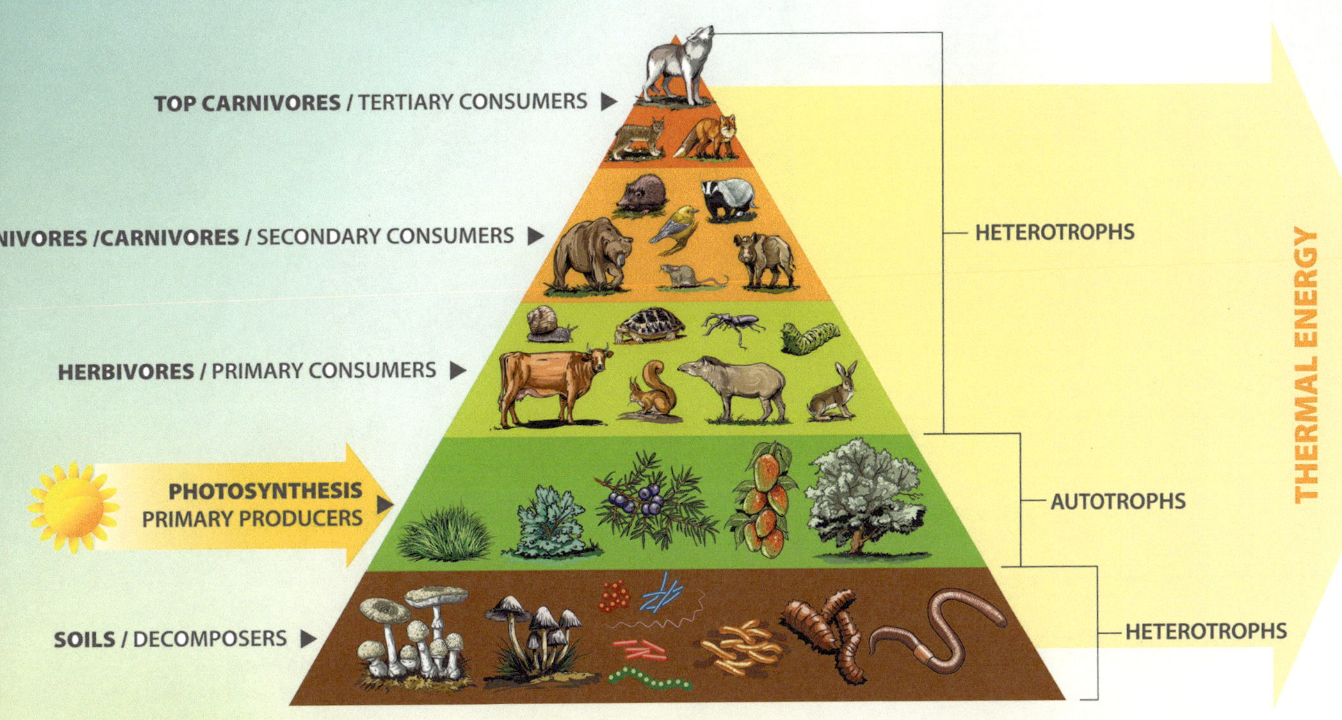

Illustration of food chain

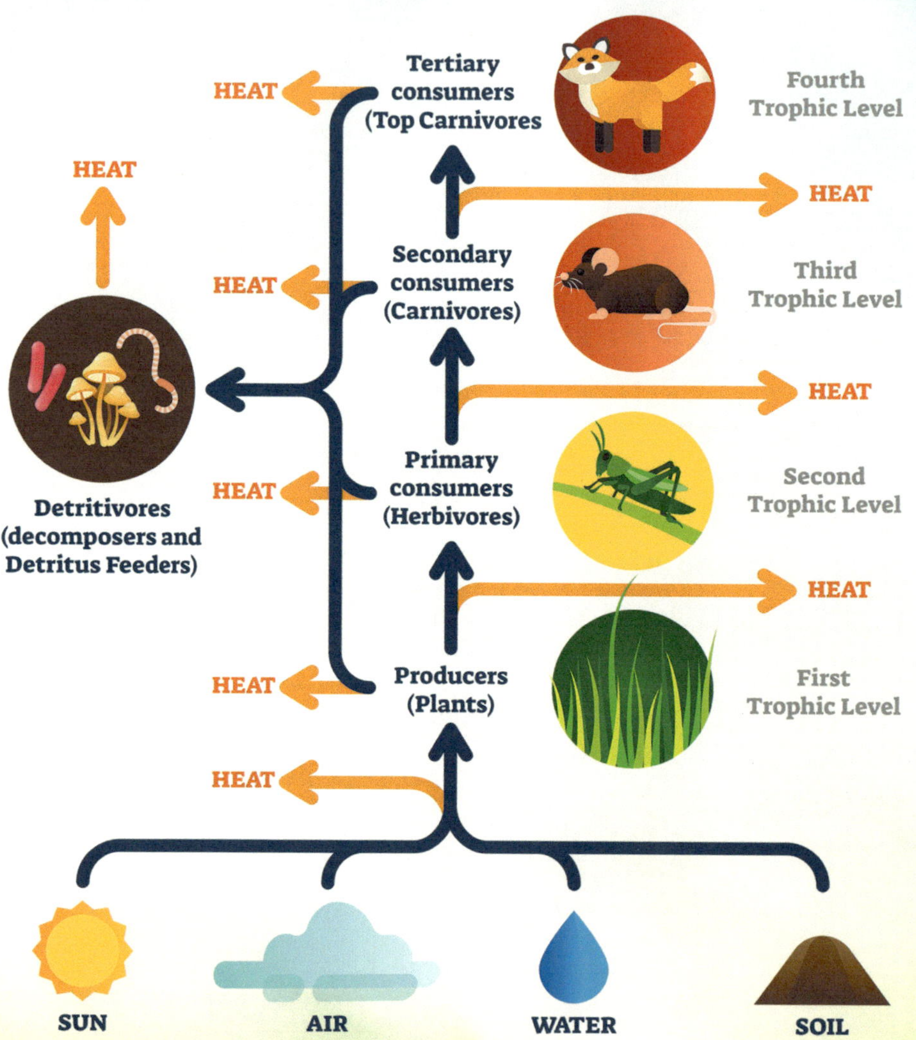

A food chain also shows the transfer of energy from the plants to the animals that eat them.

For plants to produce their own food, however, they need nutrition. This does not come from the Sun but from the soil which is formed when rocks or minerals break down. When plants pull nutrients up through their roots, they use it to grow strong. These nutrients are then passed on to the animals that eat them. Since the nutrients get passed up the food chain, the nutrients will need to go back into the soil to help new plants grow. This is done through detritivores.

Detritivores are a kind of species that eat dead organic material. Organic material is something that comes from a living creature. The detritivores break down the nutrients that are still trapped in a dead animal or fallen leaves and return them to the soil. This way the food chain can continue since more plants will be able to grow. The nutrients continue this cycle over and over. They are a non-renewable resource.

Earthworms are a good example of soil-dwelling detritivores.

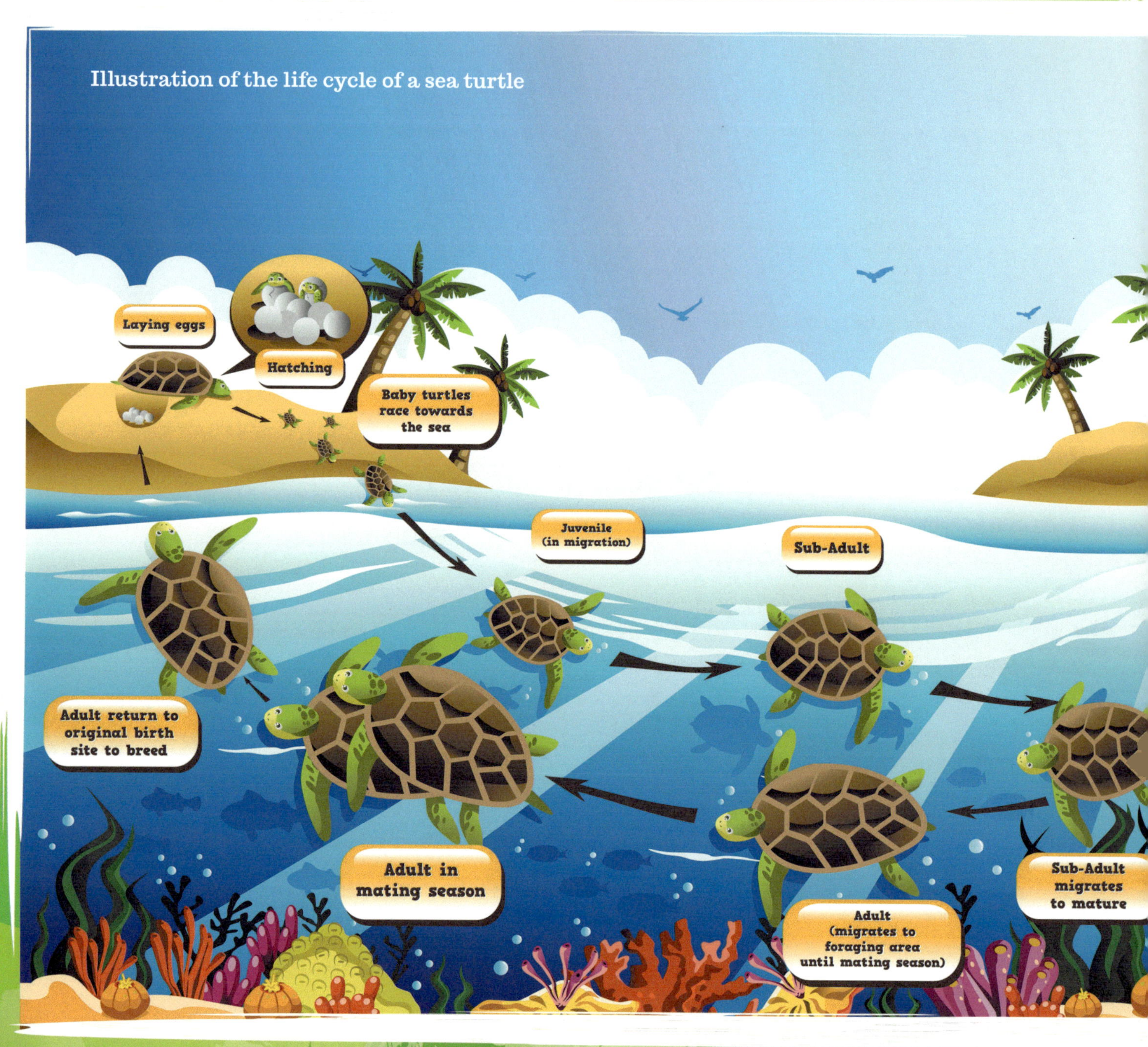
Illustration of the life cycle of a sea turtle
Laying eggs
Hatching
Baby turtles race towards the sea
Juvenile (in migration)
Sub-Adult
Adult return to original birth site to breed
Adult in mating season
Adult (migrates to foraging area until mating season)
Sub-Adult migrates to mature

Another cycle is simply the cycle of life. All living things will be born, grow, and die. However, they reproduce, and when they die their bodies will decay. They sustain the next generation who will carry the cycle forward.

Water is a non-renewable resource as well. There will always be the same amount of water on the Earth. It merely changes form.

The water cycle begins with evaporation. As the Sun heats up the water, some of the water molecules become hot enough to break off from the liquid form and rise as gas into the air. When they get high enough in the atmosphere, they will condense to form clouds. Eventually, the clouds will get too heavy and the water will return to the Earth as rain.

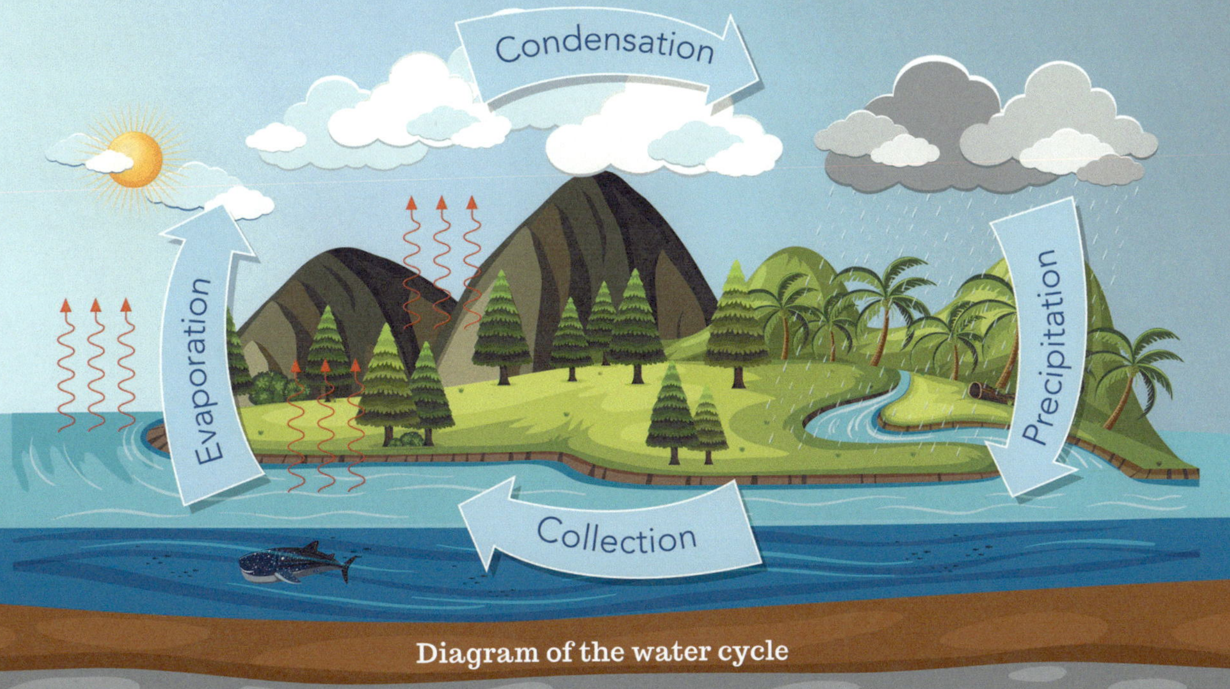

Diagram of the water cycle

When the water cycle is disturbed, it can lead to flash floods.

Water shortage and drought

The water cycle helps keep things alive by providing water in the form of rain or streams to sustain plant and animal life. When the water cycle is disturbed, it can lead to unpleasant consequences like drought or flash floods.

Chapter Three:

When Things are out of Balance

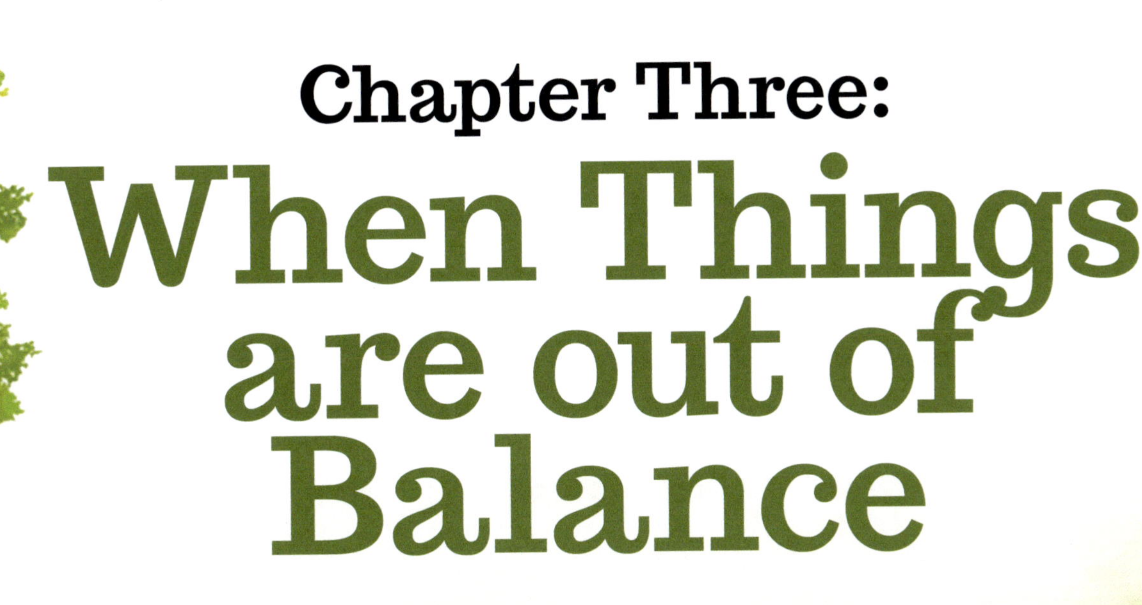

Nature always tries to balance itself when change occurs. If there is an overpopulation of predators, for example, they will eat up all the prey. This will cause competition in the predators, and some may starve. This will drive the population down again, until a healthy balance is restored. Sometimes, change can be so significant it results in a change of ecosystem. The original balance cannot be restored and so a new one is found. When this happens due to unnatural means, however, it can cause numerous problems.

Three wolves and a brown bear fighting over a carcass.

NATURAL DISASTERS

Natural Change:

Change in an ecosystem usually happens gradually. For instance, a natural disaster could decimate or totally destroy a forest. This devastation would mean that many creatures that live in the trees would have to move. This is called a push factor. A push factor is what causes an animal to leave.

After so many animals leave to find a new area to live that suits their needs, other animals who perhaps preyed on those species, or relied on those species would be forced to move as well. This would be called a pull factor. A pull factor is what might draw a species to a new location.

Animals leave to find a new area to live that suits their needs.

In time, the new ecosystems will adapt and find a new balance.

Some species might benefit from the migration of all the different species. Perhaps they will become more abundant. This might cause them to suffer from over-population. Conversely, it might draw new predators or new species to the area. A region without forest is a good habitat for other kinds of species. In time, the new ecosystems will adapt and find a new balance.

Habitat Destruction:

Natural changes to ecosystems usually happen over a long period of time. However, humans have been the cause of rapid and devastating change that has destroyed many ecosystems. As a result, some animal and plant species have gone extinct.

Humans have been the cause of rapid and devastating change that has destroyed many ecosystems.

Tree stumps after deforestation located around Alpine lake in Austria.

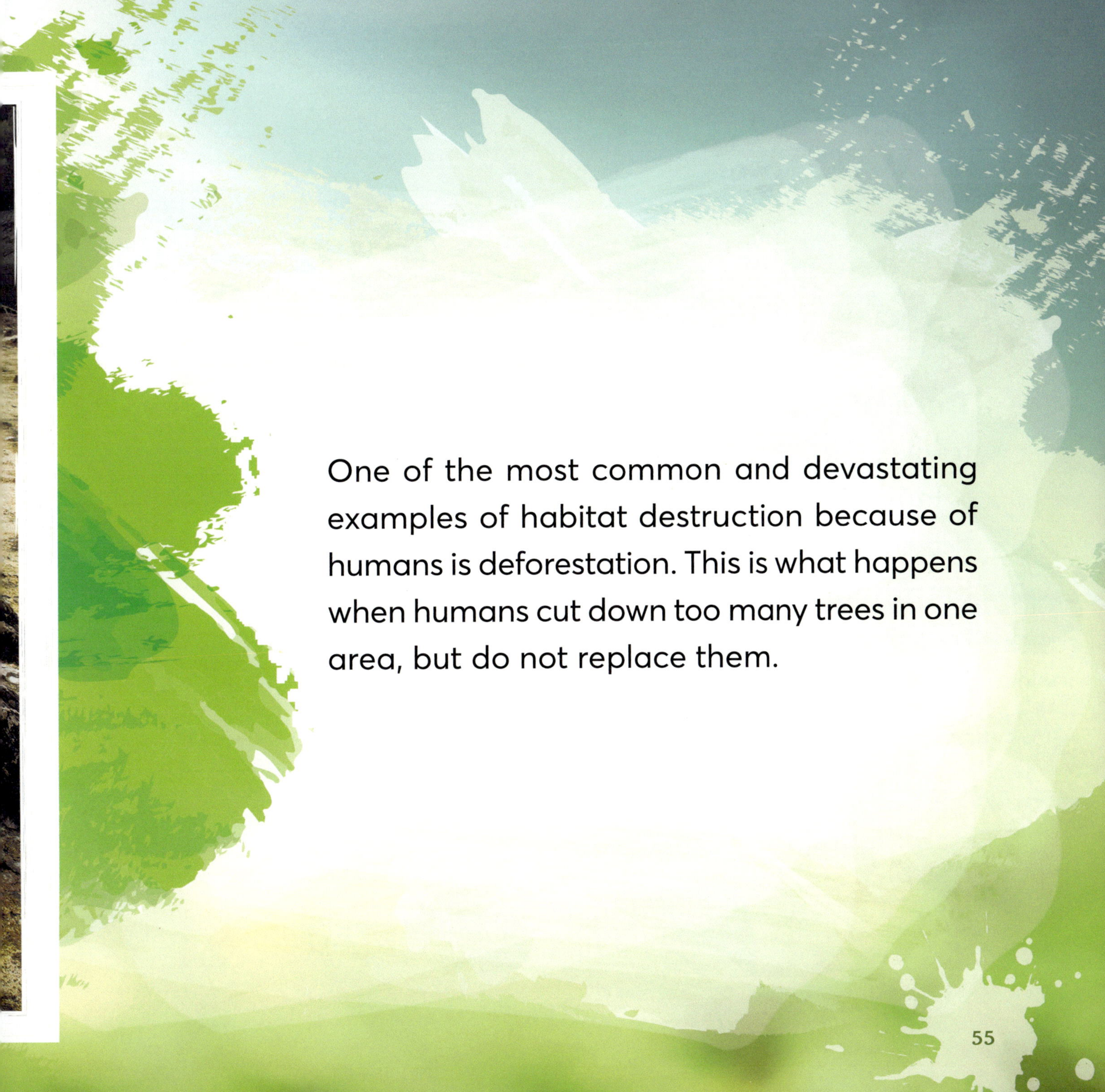

One of the most common and devastating examples of habitat destruction because of humans is deforestation. This is what happens when humans cut down too many trees in one area, but do not replace them.

Trees not only provide places for animals to live, they breathe in carbon dioxide and release oxygen into the air. Since we do the opposite, we live in harmony providing breathable air for each other. If too many trees are cut down, we risk polluting our atmosphere even more.

Trees breathe in carbon dioxide and release oxygen into the air.

Water spills over the top of Englebright Dam on the Yuba River in California, USA.

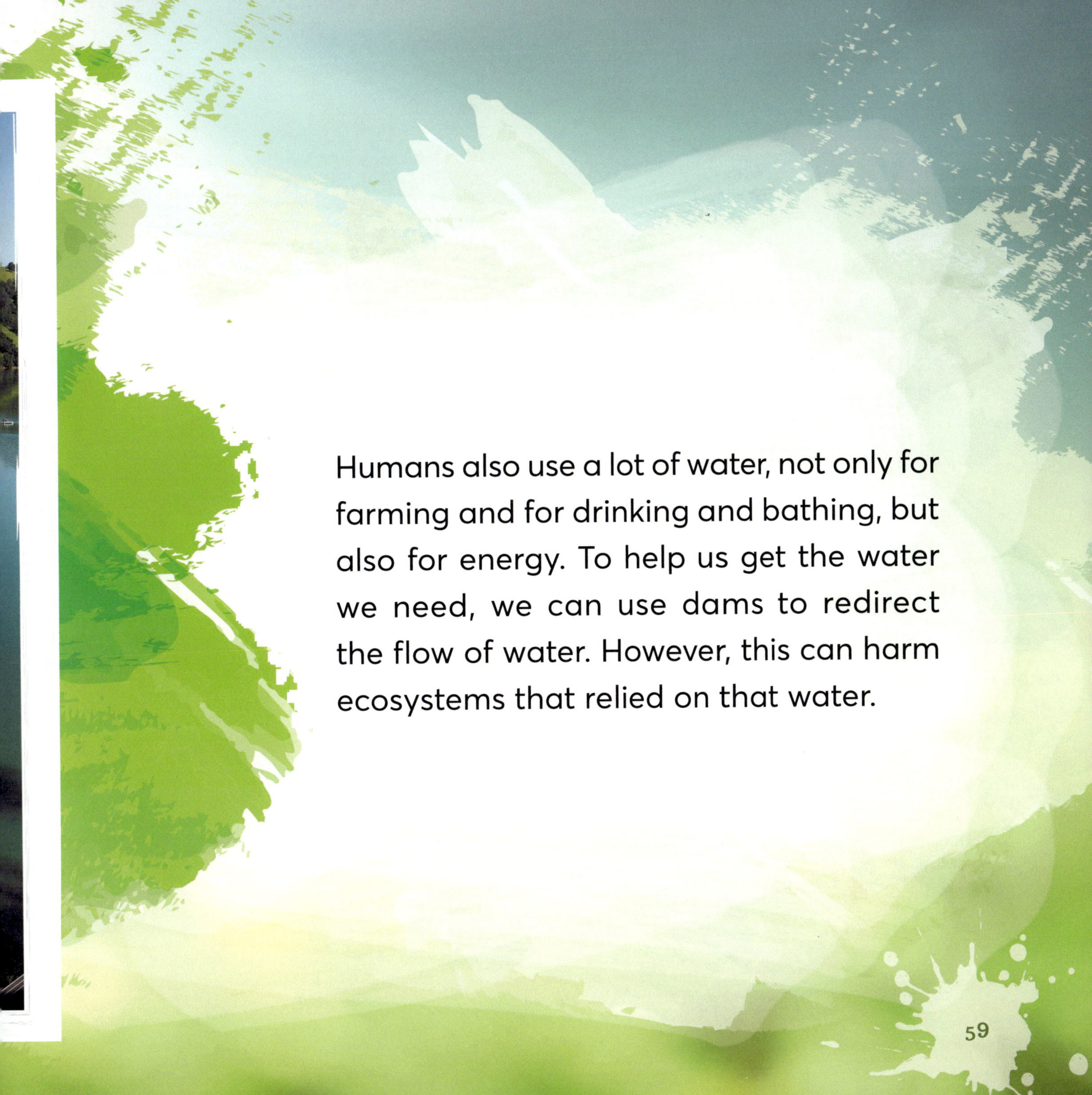

Humans also use a lot of water, not only for farming and for drinking and bathing, but also for energy. To help us get the water we need, we can use dams to redirect the flow of water. However, this can harm ecosystems that relied on that water.

Since these changes happen so quickly and over such vast areas, it is hard for the local animal and plant species to recover or adapt. This can cause many plants and animals to go extinct. Since we too are a part of an ecosystem, this indirectly harms us as well. We are a part of the balance and if we cause destruction of an ecosystem, we will suffer as well.

Abrupt changes to ecosystems can cause many plants and animals to go extinct.

Now that biologists have pointed out the dangers of not respecting the environment and its ecosystems, people are becoming more careful. Laws have been passed to protect wildlife, and recycling is being promoted. We need to remember how to live in harmony.

Recently, laws have been passed to protect wildlife.

A local community had grown and bought up a great deal of land and built houses on it.

Owls and Humans:

An interesting example of recognizing a problematic impact on the environment, and then fixing it, happened in a farming community. The local community had grown and bought up a great deal of land and built houses on it. The wide, open area seemed perfect for the needs of the people in the community. However, this open space was also the perfect hunting ground for barn owls.

As the community became more settled, they realized that there were far too many mice around. Now that the barn owls no longer had any room to hunt, and there were no longer barns to build nests in, there were no owls left to keep the population of mice in check! Things were out of balance and the ecosystem had become unhealthy.

As the community became more settled, they realized that there were far too many mice around.

The barn owls were encouraged, and they came back to keep the mice in check once more.

The people in the town were able to come up with a clever solution. They built boxes where owls could nest. They also left their garages open so that owls could come in and hunt. The owls were encouraged, and they came back to keep the mice in check once more.

There are many ecosystems on Earth. There is a natural balance that occurs in them which keeps them healthy. Sometimes, the balance is disrupted. When this happens, and it is due to negative actions of people, the consequences can be devastating. It is important that we respect the Earth, for in so doing, we respect ourselves.

Visit
www.speedypublishing.com
To view and download free content
on your favorite subject and browse
our catalog of new and exciting
books for readers of all ages.

Made in the USA
Columbia, SC
14 January 2024